Ankylosaurus

by Daniel Cohen

Consultant:
Brent Breithaupt
Director
Geological Museum
University of Wyoming

Bridgestone Books
an imprint of Capstone Press
Mankato, Minnesota

Bridgestone Books are published by Capstone Press
151 Good Counsel Drive, P.O. Box 669, Mankato, Minnesota 56002
http://www.capstone-press.com

Library of Congress Cataloging-in-Publication Data
Cohen, Daniel, 1936–
    Ankylosaurus / by Daniel Cohen.
    p. cm.—(Discovering dinosaurs)
    Summary: Describes what is known about the physical characteristics, behavior, and
habitat of this armor-plated dinosaur.
    Includes bibliographical references and index.
    ISBN 0-7368-1619-4 (hardcover)
    1. Ankylosaurus—Juvenile literature. [1. Ankylosaurus. 2. Dinosaurs.] I. Title.
QE862.O65 C6 2003
567.915—dc21   2002010551

Editorial Credits
Erika Shores, editor; Karen Risch, product planning editor; Linda Clavel, series designer;
    Patrick D. Dentinger, cover production designer; Angi Gahler, production artist;
    Alta Schaffer, photo researcher

Photo Credits
American Museum of Natural History/A. E. Anderson, 16
Corbis/Richard T. Nowitz, 4; Paul A. Souders, 8
Index Stock Imagery/RO-MA Stock, 6
Michael F. Shores, cover, 1
The Natural History Museum, 10, 20; Orbis, 14
Tom Stack & Associates/Brian Parker, 12

1 2 3 4 5 6 08 07 06 05 04 03

Table of Contents

Ankylosaurus compared to a
5-foot-tall (1.5-meter-tall) human

Ankylosaurus

Ankylosaurus (an-KY-low-SORE-us) means "stiffened reptile." This dinosaur had thick, oval plates covering its body. Ankylosaurus was about 25 to 35 feet (7.6 to 10.7 meters) long. It weighed 3 to 4 tons (2.7 to 3.6 metric tons).

The World of Ankylosaurus

Ankylosaurus lived 70 million years ago. Earth looked different during the time of Ankylosaurus. The climate was warm and wet. Many kinds of flowering plants covered the land when Ankylosaurus lived.

climate
the usual weather in a place

Edmontonia was a relative of
Ankylosaurus. Both Ankylosaurus
and Edmontonia were ankylosaurids.

Relatives of Ankylosaurus

Ankylosaurus belonged to a group
of armor-plated dinosaurs called
ankylosaurids. These dinosaurs had
tail clubs. They used the heavy club at
the end of their tail for protection.
Edmontonia (ED-mon-toh-NEE-uh)
was an ankylosaurid.

armor

the spines, plates, or bones
covering the body of some dinosaurs;
armor protected the dinosaur.

tail club

eyelids

Parts of Ankylosaurus

Ankylosaurus was one of the largest ankylosaurids. It stood on four short legs. Spikes stuck out from its head. Bony eyelids protected the dinosaur's eyes. Its tail had a club on the end.

What Ankylosaurus Ate

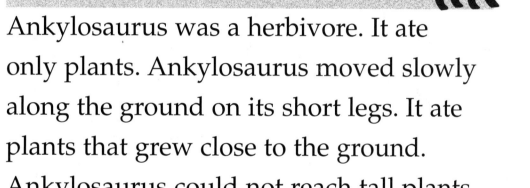

Ankylosaurus was a herbivore. It ate
only plants. Ankylosaurus moved slowly
along the ground on its short legs. It ate
plants that grew close to the ground.
Ankylosaurus could not reach tall plants
or the leaves on trees.

Predators

Dinosaurs such as Tyrannosaurus rex (ty-RAN-oh-SORE-us REX) may have hunted Ankylosaurus. Some scientists think Ankylosaurus could have hit predators with its tail club.

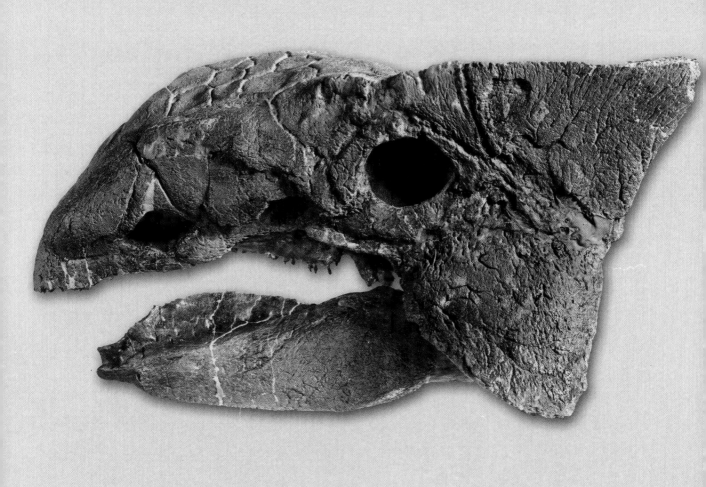

End of Ankylosaurus

Armored dinosaurs like Ankylosaurus lived until the end of the age of dinosaurs. About 65 million years ago all dinosaurs died out. Scientists are not sure why dinosaurs became extinct.

extinct
no longer living anywhere in the world

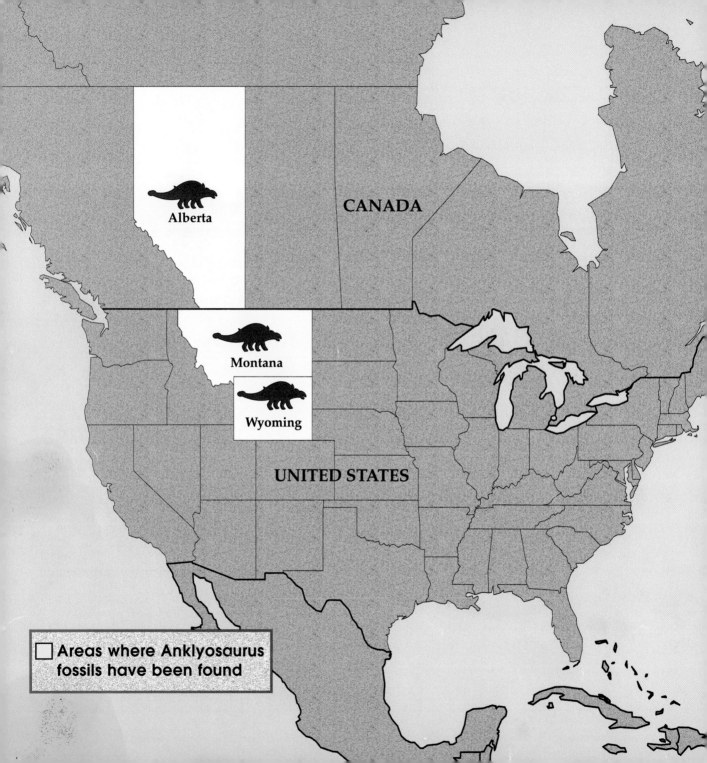

CANADA

Alberta

Montana

Wyoming

UNITED STATES

Areas where Anklyosaurus
fossils have been found

Discovering Ankylosaurus

Ankylosaurus and other armored
dinosaurs first were discovered in
western North America. In 1908,
Barnum Brown named and described
Ankylosaurus fossils from Montana.

Studying Ankylosaurus Today

Paleontologists continue to study Ankylosaurus and its relatives. Some scientists think Ankylosaurus could not move its tail side to side. Other scientists think it could. Ankylosaurus may have had large muscles to help swing its heavy, powerful tail.

Hands On: Armored Fruit

Ankylosaurus was an armored dinosaur. Its armored skin protected it from predators. Only the underside of this dinosaur was unprotected. Try this activity to see how some kinds of fruit are similar to Ankylosaurus.

What You Need

An adult to help
Watermelon
Orange
Lemon
Knife

What You Do

1. Gather a watermelon, an orange, and a lemon. Try tapping and poking the three kinds of fruit. Can your finger poke through to the inside of the fruit?
2. Ask an adult to cut a piece of watermelon, orange, and lemon.
3. Now, try poking the inside of each fruit. Can your finger poke through the soft part of the fruit?

Ankylosaurus had armor that protected its body. The outside of a fruit protects its soft inside in the same way. You can poke through the soft inside of the fruit much like a predator might have attacked the underside of an Ankylosaurus.

Words to Know

climate (KLYE-mit)—the usual weather in a place

dinosaur (DYE-na-sore)—an extinct land reptile; dinosaurs lived on Earth for more than 150 million years.

fossil (FOSS-uhl)—the remains or traces of something that once lived; bones and footprints can be fossils.

herbivore (HUR-buh-vor)—an animal that eats plants

paleontologist (PAY-lee-on-TOL-ah-jist)—a scientist who finds and studies fossils

predator (PRED-uh-tur)—an animal that hunts other animals

reptile (REP-tile)—a cold-blooded animal with a backbone; scales cover a reptile's body.

scientist (SYE-uhn-tist)—a person who studies the world around us

Read More

Benton, Michael. *Armored Giants.* Awesome Dinosaurs. Brookfield, Conn.: Copper Beech Books, 2001.

Goecke, Michael P. *Ankylosaurus.* A Buddy Book. Edina, Minn.: Abdo, 2002.

Schomp, Virginia. *Ankylosaurus and Other Armored Plant-Eaters.* Dinosaurs. New York: Benchmark Books, 2002.

Internet Sites

Track down many sites about Ankylosaurus.
Visit the FACT HOUND at *http://www.facthound.com*

IT IS EASY! IT IS FUN!

1) Go to *http://www.facthound.com*
2) Type in: 0736816194
3) Click on "FETCH IT" and FACT HOUND will find several links hand-picked by our editors.

Relax and let our pal FACT HOUND do the research for you!

Index